A tree timeline

390 million years ago

Tall plants with woody stems, roots and leaves appear – these are the first trees.

7000 BCE

To create farmland for growing crops, Stone Age hunter-gatherers begin to clear forests using fire.

700

The Japanese begin growing dwarf trees in containers, an art form known as bonsai.

500,000 BCE

The first wooden spears are made for hunting.

c. 60 CE

Ancient Greek doctor Pedanius Dioscorides writes a guide to plant medicines. It is used for the next 1,500 years!

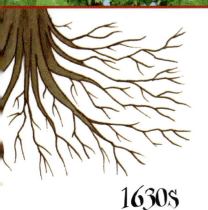

1800

Queen Charlotte of England introduces one of the first Christmas trees at Windsor Castle. Nuts, raisins, fruits and toys are hung from the branches.

1630s

Dutch scientist Jan Baptist van Helmont discovers that trees use water to help them grow, rather than 'eating' soil.

2015

In Turin, Italy, 150 trees are built into a five-story apartment block to filter air pollution, reduce traffic noise and reduce heating and cooling costs.

1779

Jan Ingenhousz, a British biologist, discovers that green leaves use energy from the sun to make food, a process known as photosynthesis.

1905

President Theodore Roosevelt creates the United States Forest Service to conserve the United States' forests.

What do trees do for us?

Save water
Their shade helps to keep lawns and fields cool, slowing down evaporation.

Clean the air
A mature tree removes almost 70 times more pollution than a newly planted tree.

Keep us cool
A young, healthy tree has the same cooling effect as 10 room-sized air conditioners running for 20 hours a day.

Absorb carbon
An acre of trees can absorb as much carbon in one year as a car produces while driving 41,000 kilometres (26,000 miles).

Keep us clean
Over 25,000 trees are cut down every day, just to make toilet paper.

Save energy
By providing shade, trees planted in the right place can lower energy bills by up to 50 percent.

Produce the oxygen we breathe
An acre of trees can supply enough oxygen for eight people every day.

Author:

Jim Pipe studied ancient and modern history at Oxford University and spent 10 years in publishing before becoming a full-time writer. He has written numerous nonfiction books for children, many on historical subjects. He lives in Dublin, Ireland, with his wife and sons.

Artist:

Mark Bergin was born in Hastings, England, in 1961. He studied at Eastbourne College of Art and specialises in historical reconstructions, aviation and maritime subjects. He lives in Bexhill-on-Sea with his wife and children.

Series creator:

David Salariya was born in Dundee, Scotland. He has illustrated a wide range of books and has created and designed many new series for publishers in the UK and overseas. David established The Salariya Book Company in 1989. He lives in Brighton with his wife, illustrator Shirley Willis, and their son Jonathan.

Editor: **Jacqueline Ford**

Editorial Assistant: **Mark Williams**

Published in Great Britain in MMXVII by
Book House, an imprint of
The Salariya Book Company Ltd
25 Marlborough Place, Brighton BN1 1UB
www.salariya.com

ISBN: 978-1-911242-31-4

SALARIYA
SCRIBO BOOK HOUSE SCRIBBLERS

3 5 7 9 8 6 4 2

A CIP catalogue record for this book is available from the British Library.
Printed and bound in Malaysia.
Reprinted in MMXIX.

Visit
www.salariya.com
for our online catalogue and
free fun stuff.

PAPER FROM
SUSTAINABLE
FORESTS

You Wouldn't Want to Live Without™
Trees!

Written by
Jim Pipe

Illustrated by
Mark Bergin

Series created by
David Salariya

BOOK HOUSE
a SALARIYA *imprint*

Contents

Introduction

Trees are natural wonders, growing from small seeds you can hold in your hand into green giants bigger than a house. They are rugged survivors that can live for hundreds or even thousands of years. Found in baking deserts, icy arctic regions and salty swamps, many trees fight a daily battle against drought, floods, pests or predators. At the same time, they provide us with essential things such as fuel, food and shelter. Many of the products we use every day are made from trees, such as paper, books, grocery bags and toilet paper. Trees even produce the oxygen that we breathe. Just imagine a world without trees…it would be a barren, dry and toxic wasteland! You really wouldn't want to live without trees.

TREES PROVIDE FOOD for humans and animals, protect the soil with their roots, and clean the air with their leaves and bark. They're also a cool place to hang out on a hot day!

Why hug a tree?

Trees and humans go back a long, long way. For thousands of years, trees have provided us with fruits and nuts to eat, as well as wood for fuel, building and transport. Imagine what our past would have been like without them! Many people say their favourite landscape is a grassy plain dotted with trees. Perhaps we like trees because we're built in a similar way: upright with a bushy top and limbs sticking out from a central trunk.

He's barking up the wrong tree!

SLEEP TIGHT.
Is your bedroom upstairs? Many people like to sleep up high. Perhaps it's because human ancestors slept in the trees to avoid predators at night.

I feel so ancient!

I feel so small!

Top tip

Research shows that playgrounds with trees make children happier and healthier – so you don't even have to hug a tree to feel better!

HOLY WOOD. Because of their height, great age and silence, forests often feel spiritual. In ancient times, people believed wooden objects such as wands and staffs were magical.

HANDY HUMANS. Our dextrous hands are the result of our distant ancestors spending 80 million years in the trees. When primates started to walk upright on two legs – a feature of the earliest humans – they learned to put their hands to other uses, such as making and using tools.

Look, no hands.

PEOPLE AND TREES are alike on the inside, too: our arteries and veins look like roots and branches!

LIVING ICONS. Long-living trees, a symbol of power and history, are often found on banknotes and coins. This American quarter shows a bristlecone pine in the Nevada Great Basin National Park.

11

What is a tree?

In many ways, trees are just like many other plants, with roots, leaves, flowers and fruits. But their woody trunks allow them to grow tall and lift their leaves high into the sky. Without trees, our world would seem a lot flatter! To help them grow tall, trees are anchored to the ground by strong underground roots, which also provide them with food. This stable foundation allows them to grow and spread their spindly branch tops up into the sky, sometimes over 30 stories high!

POWER TOWER. A tree's green leaves contain chlorophyll, a chemical that soaks up energy from sunlight. Carbon dioxide in the air enters the leaves through openings called stomas. The chlorophyll and carbon dioxide react with water sucked up by the roots to create oxygen.

When I grow up I want to be a book.

GROWTH SPURT. As a tree grows from a seedling into a sapling, it develops a trunk and branches with stiff, woody cells at the centre.

That tickles!

HAIRY SUCKERS. Trees have smaller side roots that sprout out from a thick central root. These side roots are covered in millions of tiny 'hairs' that can suck in hundreds of litres of water a day. Trees growing next to each other can also exchange nutrients and water through their roots.

Only between 1 and 10 percent of a tree is actually alive. The centre of a tree – the heartwood – is made up of dead tubes. Around this is the sapwood, made up of living tubes that bring up water from the roots.

Heartwood

Sapwood

TRUNK ROUTE. A trunk is made up of a closely packed bundle of tubes that carry water up to the leaves, and sugars down to the roots. The trunk never stops growing, thanks to a thin layer called the cambium. Over 50 years, a tree in Washington, USA grew right around a bicycle that had been left locked to it!

Who needs an umbrella?

FIREPROOF. A tree's dead outer bark protects it against insects, disease, ice, storms and fire. The bark of a Douglas fir can withstand fires up to 650 degrees Celsius (1,200 degrees Fahrenheit)!

BELIEVE IT OR NOT. The world's largest tree, the sequoia, has scaly leaves the size of a fingernail. African raffia palms can grow leaves over 25 metres (82 feet) long – the same length as a blue whale!

Why do trees rule?

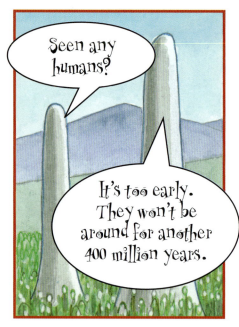

Seen any humans?

It's too early. They won't be around for another 400 million years.

In the plant world, it pays to be big. Trees are the bullies of the natural world, hogging the sunlight and reaching deep down into the earth for water and minerals. To protect themselves, they've evolved all sorts of ways to ward off pests and disease, from prickly holly leaves to the chemicals in cedar trees that help defend against fungi and rot. Although they can't move around, these wooden giants can scatter millions of their seeds at a time, spreading them far and wide. It is no surprise that there are 3 trillion trees on Earth, which cover a third of our planet's land in forests.

TO DISCOVER A WORLD without trees, you'd need to travel back in time to Earth over 400 million years ago, when our planet was dotted in giant fungi up to 8 metres (26 feet) tall!

FLOWER POWER. Ash trees are dioecious, which means there are usually separate male and female trees. Pollination happens when the wind carries pollen from the male trees to the female trees. Both male and female flowers are purple and appear before the leaves in spring, growing in spiked clusters at the tips of twigs.

NATURE'S HELPERS. Trees use bees, birds, bats, and even giraffes to carry pollen for them, attracting them with bright colours or tempting them with sweet nectar or fruits. In apple and almond orchards, millions of bees are brought in to help pollination.

These guys are the bee's knees.

But I don't have any knees...?

3. Flowers form clusters

2. Flowers emerge

1. Buds appear

Nuts! I know it's here somewhere!

TASTY PARCELS.
Pinecones, apples, acorns, cherries, and prickly horse chestnut cases are all fruits that protect the seeds they carry. Animals eat the tasty treats, then scatter the seeds through their droppings as they move around. Squirrels plant seeds by accident: they bury acorns to store them, but sometimes don't retrieve all of them!

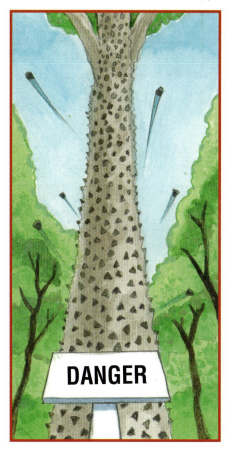

The roots of stilt palms grow sideways as well as down, so these trees can 'walk' into gaps in the forest. They can move up to 2 metres (6.5 feet) in three years.

FAR-FLUNG FLOATERS.
Sycamore seeds are shaped like papery wings. They whirl through the air like tiny helicopters.

Yuck! This one's gone off.

CHEMICAL WARFARE. Orange and lemon trees fight off beetles, grasshoppers and flies with chemicals called limonoids. The toxic manchineel tree in Florida causes painful blisters if you stand under it in the rain!

DANGER

BACK OFF! The exploding fruit of the sandbox tree can hurl seeds at over 200 kilometres per hour (124 miles per hour).

15

All shapes and sizes

The world would look very flat and boring if it weren't covered in woods and forests. There are around 60,000 known tree species and we're still discovering more, because some are hidden deep in tropical forests. There are many distinctive and recognisable tree shapes, from drooping weeping willows to the bent and twisted trees found on windswept mountaintops. However, most trees belong to one of two groups: broadleaves, which have wide and flat leaves; or conifers, which have needlelike leaves and seeds packed into cones.

Are we there yet?

SCIENTISTS EXPLORE the tallest and most remote trees using hot-air balloons, treetop walkways, giant construction cranes – or simply by climbing them!

BROADLEAF trees, such as oaks and maples, have large flat leaves that soak up sunlight. They are deciduous, which means they lose their leaves in the autumn. The leaves often turn yellow, orange or red before they are shed.

Common tree shapes

Oval
(Sugar maple)

Layered
(Acacia)

Vase (Elm)

Pyramidal
(Douglas Fir)

Round
(White Ash)

Columnar
(Cypress)

Stubby
(Hawthorn)

Weeping
(Weeping Willow)

Broad (Oak)

You can do it!

In busy town centres, look out for trees with their branches chopped off near the main trunk. This cutting, known as pollarding, is done to control a tree's height.

CONIFERS such as pines and fir trees have thin, needlelike leaves. They can survive in cold or dry areas where broadleaves can't. Most are evergreen and shed leaves throughout the year.

PALM TREES are found all over the world, from deserts to rain forests. The Quindío wax palm can grow over 60 metres (200 feet) tall.

A home to hundreds

When you cut down a tree, it's like knocking down an apartment building. A single oak tree can support hundreds of bug species. These provide food for birds and small mammals, while dozens of other species – including wild boar, pigeons, ducks, squirrels, badgers and deer – feed on an oak's acorns. Trees also shelter animals from the sun and wind. In the icy tundra, short trees are a refuge for marmots, which fertilise the trees with their droppings. On the African savanna, acacia trees provide shelter and shade for nesting birds.

Insects lay eggs on tree bark because it provides a ready source of food when their young hatch. Deer rub their antlers on bark to sharpen them, and bears rub against it to scratch an itch!

Armies of creepy-crawlies live hidden among a tree's roots. Earthworms draw air and dead leaves down from the surface as they wriggle underground, putting nutrients back into the soil.

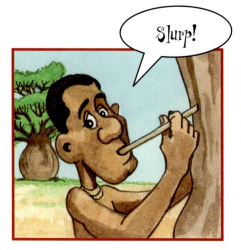

Slurp!

AFRICAN BAOBAB TREES have hollow insides that can hold over 110,000 litres (30,000 gallons) of water. The San people of the Kalahari Desert suck water from them using reed straws.

HANGERS ON. Branches and trunks are home to epiphytes, which are plants that grow on other plants.

Trees can survive even when the heartwood has rotted away, as long as the sapwood and cambium survive. When you knock on a hollow tree, the louder the sound, the more hollow it is.

Centipedes and small mammals such as shrews hunt for worms, spiders, flies and other small prey among fallen leaves and fungi at the bottom of trees.

SURPRISE VISITORS. On Maud Island in New Zealand, little blue penguins nest in the forest at night. In the Pacific islands, giant robber crabs climb up trees and drop coconuts to crack them open.

ADVENTUROUS EATERS. In southwest Morocco, goats love the fruit of argan trees so much that they've learnt to climb them!

Can I have some more?

Sorry, I'm shellfish!

19

Lungs of the planet

Without trees, life as we know it just couldn't exist. An acre of trees produces enough oxygen for eight people to breathe for a whole year. No wonder the Amazon rainforest is known as the lungs of the planet! Forests feed oxygen and minerals into the ocean and also act as a heat shield, cooling our planet. They provide a home for 80 percent of the world's plants and land animals. Around 300 million people live in forests around the world, and over 1.5 billion people depend on them to make a living.

DANGER FLOODING

TROPICAL RAINFORESTS grow in very hot, damp places. The trees are packed so tightly that the forest floor is as dark as night, and most animals live in the upper branches. When the Amazon river floods, covering some trees, fish feed on fruit and river dolphins race through branches.

MANGROVE SWAMPS are forests of trees that can survive in the salty, muddy waters where rivers meet the sea. They're home to animals such as saltwater crocodiles, fiddler crabs and crab-eating monkeys.

How it works

Rainforests are divided into four layers:

Emergent: Tops of the tallest trees

Canopy: Upper branches and leaves

Understory: Small trees or bushes

Forest floor: Soil, dead plants, and small ferns

TEMPERATE FORESTS grow in regions where it rarely gets very hot or very cold. Sunlight easily reaches the forest floor, allowing flowers and mosses to grow. Forests of oak, ash and chestnut trees provide a home for deer, squirrels and wild boar.

TAIGA. In these cold northern forests, winters are long and harsh. The trees here are mostly evergreen species such as spruce, fir and pine. Their sloping shape allows snow to slide off easily, so their branches don't break from the snow's weight.

STARTING OVER. When a patch of forest is destroyed by flood or fire, it takes about 60 years for the same plant species to reappear. That's one reason it's important to take care of trees!

1. Weeds and grasses start to grow first.

2. Dying shrubs add nutrients to the soil.

3. Young forest of small trees emerges.

4. Large broadleaf trees take over.

21

The wonder of wood

People have been making things out of wood since the earliest humans used branches as clubs. Cheap, strong and beautiful to look at, wood is an incredibly versatile material. Timber for houses or furniture comes from trees sawn in a lumber mill. The bark is used for resins, waxes and adhesives. Wood chips and sawdust are boiled with chemicals until they turn into pulp, which is then squeezed and dried to make paper.

CEDARVILLE. The Native peoples of Vancouver Island, Canada, built longhouses from thick planks of cedar wood. They carved tree trunks into canoes and totem poles, and made clothes by pounding bark into fibres, which they then wove together.

Speech bubble: Who pulled the plug?

You can do it!

We use things made from wood every day. From matchsticks to magazines, take a look around your house and see how many wooden objects your family uses.

LET'S GO! For 10,000 years, wood has kept people on the move, from Roman chariots to Viking longships and pirate galleons.

Speech bubble: I wish someone would hurry up and invent marshmallows!

CORK from the spongy bark of cork oak trees is used for fishing floats, roofs, beehives and bulletin boards. The Portuguese Whistler tree produces enough corks for 100,000 wine bottles!

FIREWOOD was our very first source of energy, and many people worldwide still use it for cooking and heating.

CITY ON STILTS. The islands of Venice, Italy, were built on a foundation of tree trunks. Over 1,200 years later, those same trunks still support almost all of central Venice.

'Wood' you believe it?

There's a lot more to wood than wood! Wood is made up of tiny fibres called cellulose, and the natural glue that holds them together, called lignin. Cellulose is released when wood chips are turned into pulp. It can be used to make things such as rocket fuel, explosives, nail polish and toilet seats! Lignin is also used for making many things, from paints and dyes to plastics (such as the celluloid in old photographic film) and fertilisers.

WOOD BY-PRODUCTS are found in everything from hairspray to artificial vanilla flavouring. There are even wood products in our clothes – in man-made materials such as rayon – as well as in vitamin pills, toothpaste and shampoo.

Furniture

Rocket fuel

Toothpaste

Soft drinks

Cleaning products

Aspirin

Hairspray

Fertilisers

Rayon

Cork

Deodorants

Cosmetics

Vitamins

Spices

Ceramics

Chewing gum

FRUITFUL. In addition to a huge variety of fruits and nuts, trees give us spices such as nutmeg and cinnamon. Chewing gum is made from tree sap, and the dried seeds of the kola tree were once used in soft drinks. A single maple tree can produce up to 100 litres (26 gallons) of sweet syrup in a single season.

Top tip

Doctors have found that patients who can see trees from their hospital window usually recover faster than those who can't.

IN THE BATHROOM
• Cellulose gives lipstick its smooth texture.
• Tree gum is used in making sticking plasters.
• Traditionally, people in India used twigs from the Neem tree to clean and whiten their teeth.

AIR FRESHENER. Ancient Egyptian priests burned sweet-smelling woods to try to cover up rotten odours as they made corpses into mummies.

FOREST MEDICINES. Aspirin was originally produced from willow bark. Quinine from the cinchona tree, found in the Andes mountains of South America, was once used to treat the tropical disease malaria.

25

Nature's clocks

Trees show the passing of time unlike anything else in nature. Just watch how they change with the seasons: the buds and blossoms of spring, the rich deep greens of summer, the yellows, reds, and browns of autumn, and the bare branches of winter. If you look at a tree stump, you'll see a unique pattern of rings, one for each year of the tree's life. Trees don't die of old age. They are generally killed by insects, disease or by people. California bristlecone pines and giant sequoias are regarded as the oldest trees in the world, and have been known to live for up to almost 5,000 years!

Spring

Winter

CHANGING COLOURS. In autumn, the green chemical that soaks up the sun's energy (chlorophyll) is broken down. As the green fades away, the yellow, orange and red colours of other chemicals in the leaves are revealed.

MARKING TIME. Counting the number of rings in a tree trunk will tell you how old it was when it was cut down. The wider the ring, the more a tree grew that particular year.

1969 First astronaut lands on the Moon _____

1879 Thomas Edison invents the lightbulb _____

1492 Christopher Columbus discovers America _____

950 CE Viking raids occur across Europe _____

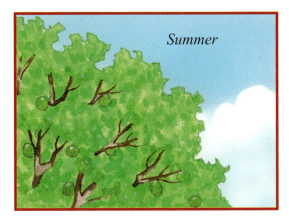

Summer

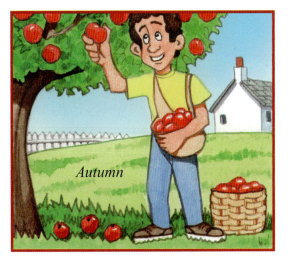

Autumn

Top tip

Trees are compasses as well as clocks. Moss grows on the northern side of the trunk, where it is shadier. Branches on the north side are also thinner and tend to grow upwards.

OLD TIMERS. A few of the gnarled bristlecone pines growing in the White Mountains of California, USA, have survived for over 4,000 years. They grow incredibly slowly, less than a quarter of a millimetre per year.

FOUR SEASONS. Broadleaf trees in temperate forests go through a cycle of four seasons:
- Spring. Buds start to unfurl into flowers, called blossoms, and fresh young leaves.
- Summer. Flowers die off and, on some trees, fruits start to grow. Leaves grow larger and wider.
- Autumn. Most broadleaf trees lose their leaves. Fruits and nuts also become ripe.
- Winter. Deciduous trees lose their leaves.

I'm not telling you my age. And no, you can't count my rings!

Sacred trees

Even in a world of towering skyscrapers, tall trees still inspire awe and wonder in humans. No wonder so many religions believe trees and woods are holy. For Hindus, the banyan tree is one of the resting places of the god Krishna, and the same tree is sacred to Buddhists. Many popular festivals are still based around trees. To celebrate the arrival of the cherry tree blossom in spring, Japanese people hold special parties known as Hanami ('flower viewing') under the trees. And would Christmas be the same without a tree?

HOLY HOLLY. Yew, holly, oak and ash trees were all sacred to the ancient Celts, who gathered in shady glades for sacred rituals. In winter, they hung holly branches in their homes to welcome in woodland spirits, believed to use the holly to shelter from the cold.

TREE SPIRITS. The ancient Greeks believed that cutting down trees killed the Dryads, the woodland spirits who lived in them. In Sweden, the wood nymph Skogsrå is a guardian of woods and wild animals.

SUPERSTITION surrounds many trees. In Jani, a Latvian festival, people hang rowan tree branches on their houses to ward off witches. Since aspen trees tremble in the wind, some people used to believe that if an illness made them shiver, they could be cured by attaching a lock of their hair to an aspen and saying a prayer.

How it works

Why do we knock on wood for good luck? This idea comes from an ancient belief that rapping on trees would bring out the helpful spirits who lived in them.

FESTIVALS. In Europe, there is a tradition of dancing around a maypole (originally a living tree), to celebrate the arrival of summer.

CHRISTMAS TREES. In 16th century Germany, pine trees were decorated with gingerbread at Christmas. Christmas trees became popular in England and the United States in the early 1800s after England's Queen Charlotte had a tree put up in Windsor Castle.

"BEWARE THE OAK, it draws the stroke!" The Vikings associated oak trees with Thor, their god of lightning – perhaps because big oaks get struck more than other trees as they are so tall.

Trees under attack!

Every year, huge areas of forest are destroyed by fires, pests, disease, extreme weather or grazing animals. At the same time, humans are wiping out trees at a terrifying pace. Over the past 8,000 years, we've already destroyed almost half of the forests that once covered half our planet. Today, an area of forest the size of a football field is logged or burned every two seconds, to make way for mines, farms or new houses.

WHEN TROPICAL FORESTS are cut down – known as deforestation – many animals lose their homes and die. The survivors move on to other areas, but it can be hard to compete with other animals already living there.

DROUGHT. Trees help to control the weather. When rain falls on a forest, new clouds are created. If huge areas of trees are cut down, rain clouds do not form, the land becomes much drier, and crops struggle to grow.

DEADLY DISEASES. Dutch elm disease has killed huge numbers of American and European elm trees. Climate change has helped cause a plague of bark beetles that carry a fungus from tree to tree.

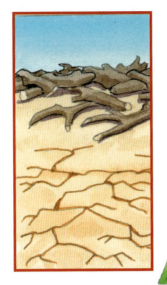

Thieves steal hundreds of millions of pounds' worth of trees every year. Park Rangers are tracking down the thieves by matching the DNA of stumps to logs at lumber mills.

This mushroom sure gets around.

Yes, he's a fungi!

GLOBAL WARMING. Destroying trees adds to climate change. Trees soak up carbon dioxide, a greenhouse gas that traps heat from the sun in the atmosphere. Without its great forests, the world would heat up like an oven.

SPECIES LOSS. Seventy percent of the world's plants and animals live in forests, and many species are losing their habitats to deforestation. Without trees, the soil is easily washed or blown away, making it hard to grow crops in what remains.

31

The future of trees

Climate change is already beginning to transform life on Earth. Around the globe, temperatures are climbing and sea levels are rising. A quarter of Earth's species could be headed for extinction by 2050. But protecting forests is one of the best ways to prevent this from happening. Replanting trees helps local communities, too: stabilising the soil, providing shade for crops, and providing firewood, fruit and nuts. The future of trees – and the planet – depends on all of us. You wouldn't want to live without them, so why not plant a tree in your school or garden?

TREES PRODUCE the oxygen we breathe, cool our planet and clean our water. Their roots prevent flooding and their leaves filter out smoke and dust from vehicles and factories. Without trees, we'd soon be living in a polluted, desertlike wasteland.

CHAMPION TREES. Scientists are now cloning some of the world's oldest and largest trees, to study why they have survived for so long. Some of the saplings are being planted in colder locations, to help them survive if our planet continues to get warmer.

You can do it!

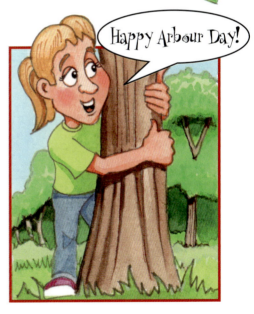

Everyone can help protect trees by treating them with respect. Reuse and recycle paper, use sustainable wood products – and plant a tree!

LET'S GET PLANTING! By planting new trees, we can solve many of the problems caused by deforestation. In the Philippines, mangroves are being replanted to help protect coastlines against tsunamis and typhoons.

Happy Arbour Day!

DIY FOREST. Over 30 years ago, teenager Jadav Payeng began planting seeds along a sandbar in India's Assam region. Today, he lives in his own island jungle inhabited by tigers, elephants and other wild animals.

ARBOUR DAY. From the Latin word *arbor*, meaning tree, Arbour Day is a special day where people are encouraged to plant and care for trees. It is celebrated in many countries around the world.

Glossary

Atmosphere The thick layer of air that surrounds the Earth.

Broadleaf A tree with wide flat leaves, sometimes known as a hardwood, that is usually deciduous.

Bud A small bump on a plant that grows into a leaf, flower or shoot.

Cambium The layer inside a tree trunk that makes it grow.

Cell The basic unit of all living things including plants and animals.

Cellulose The material that makes up the walls of a cell and fibres such as cotton.

Chlorophyll The chemical found in all green plants that soaks up energy from the sun and carbon dioxide from the air. It mixes them with water to create sugars and oxygen.

Climate change The warming of our planet due to human activities, also known as global warming.

Cloning Making an identical copy of a living thing.

Conifer A tree with cones and needle-like leaves that are usually evergreen.

Deciduous A tree that sheds its leaves in autumn.

Deforestation Clearing trees for farmland, mining or homes.

Dexterous Skilful with the hands.

Drought A long spell of very dry weather.

Epiphyte A plant that grows on another plant.

Evergreen A plant that keeps its green leaves all year.

Fungi A group of living things including mushrooms, moulds and yeast.

Heartwood The dense inner part of a tree.

Lignin A material found in wood that makes it tough and stiff.

Limonoid Strong-smelling chemicals found in lemons and oranges.

Mangrove A tree that grows in salty, muddy waters of swamps or shallow sea water.

Nectar A sugary liquid in flowers that encourages bees and birds to collect pollen from them.

Pollarding Cutting the top and branches of a tree to encourage new growth.

Pollination When the wind or animals such as bees carry pollen between flowering plants, so they can then make seeds and create new plants.

Pollution The presence of substances in the air, water or ground that make a habitat unclean, such as toxic chemicals.

Predators Animals that hunt and kill other animals for food.

Resin A yellow or brown sticky material that comes from trees that is used to make plastics and other products.

Sapling A young, thin tree.

Sapwood Soft layers of new wood between the tough inner heartwood and the bark.

Seedling A young plant.

Sustainable Able to continue indefinitely or for a long time. Sustainable forestry is when new trees are grown to replace those that are cut down.

Taiga The giant conifer forests in icy northern regions.

Temperate A mild climate that never gets very hot or very cold.

Toxic Poisonous.

Index

Trees in tales and legends

Forests have long been viewed as mysterious, dangerous, spooky and something to be conquered. They have been an important feature in many tales and legends going back thousands of years. Here are just a few examples.

- In the story of Snow White and the Seven Dwarfs, Snow White escapes from her wicked stepmother by living with the dwarfs in the middle of a forest.

- Lost in a forest, Hansel and Gretel come across a gingerbread cottage belonging to an old witch, who tries to put them in her oven.

- Little Red Riding Hood runs into a big, bad wolf in a forest while taking a basket of food to her sick grandmother.

- In the story of Beauty and the Beast, Belle's father gets lost in a forest during a storm. Looking for shelter, he enters a palace belonging to a hideous 'Beast'.

- In the 4,000-year-old *Epic of Gilgamesh*, the oldest written story of all, the heroes Gilgamesh and Enkidu travel to the Cedar Forest to fight monsters who live there.

- In Viking legends, Myrkvid is a dark and dangerous forest that even gods and heroes struggle to cross.

Top extraordinary trees

The Trembling Giant in Utah is a grove of 47,000 quaking aspen trees connected by a single root system. Covering half a square kilometre (107 acres) and weighing 6,615 tons, it is one of the world's most massive living things. At least 80,000 years old, it is also one of the oldest.

The tallest living thing is a coast redwood tree known as Hyperion, which stands in California's Redwood National Park. It is 116 metres (380 feet) tall – twice the height of the Statue of Liberty!

The General Sherman Tree in California's Sequoia National Park is the world's largest single tree by volume. This giant sequoia has an estimated volume of 1,487 cubic metres (52,513 cubic feet).

A Montezuma cypress in Oaxaca, Mexico, holds the record for the tree with the greatest girth (the distance around the trunk of the tree). It measures over 36 metres (119 feet) around – the same as ten family cars placed end to end.

A gigantic banyan tree found near Kolkata, India, covers an area about the size of a football field. It has 3,511 roots that connect to the earth, making it look like a whole forest of trees.

Did you know?

A sacred fig tree known as Jaya Sri Maha Bodhi in Anuradhapura, Sri Lanka, was planted in 288 BCE, making it the oldest living tree planted by humans.

The ginkgo tree has been around since the dinosaurs. Fossils have been found that show similar trees were alive over 170 million years ago, during the Jurassic Period.

Scientists studying an old kapok tree in the rain forests of Costa Rica found over 4,000 different species of creatures living on it, including frogs, birds and bats.

The manchineel tree that grows in Florida is perhaps the most dangerous tree in the world. It can poison water with its leaves, and its fruit – nicknamed the 'death apple'–can cause death if eaten.

The dragon blood tree gets its fearsome name from its dark red sap, which is used as a dye and as a varnish for violins.

Coconuts kill around 150 people every year. Falling from heights of up to 25 metres (80 feet), they can reach speeds of around 80 kph (50 mph) by the time they hit the ground below.

Trees on Slope Point in the far south of New Zealand grow at a strange angle and have warped, twisted branches, due to being constantly battered by powerful Antarctic winds.

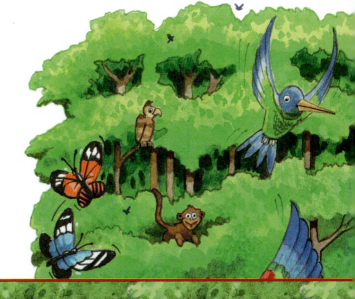